THE CIVIL WAR

LIFE GOES ON

The Civil War at Home, 1861-1865

James R. Arnold and Roberta Wiener

LERNER PUBLICATIONS COMPANY • MINNEAPOLIS

**First American edition published in 2002
by Lerner Publications Company**

The Civil War series is created and produced by Graham Beehag Books, in cooperation with Lerner Publications Company, a division of Lerner Publishing Group.

Lerner Publications Company
A division of Lerner Publishing Group
241 First Avenue North
Minneapolis, Minnesota 55401 U.S.A.

Website address: www.lernerbooks.com

Library of Congress Cataloging-in-Publication Data

Arnold, James R.
  Life goes on : the Civil War at home, 1861–1865 / by James R.
Arnold and Roberta Wiener.
      p. cm.—(The Civil War)
Includes bibliographical references and index.
  ISBN 0-8225-2315-9 (lib. bdg. : alk. paper)
  1. United States—History—Civil War, 1861–1865—Social
aspects—Juvenile literature. [1. United States—History—Civil
War, 1861–1865.] I. Wiener, Roberta, 1952– II. Title.
  E468.9 . A73   2002
  973.7'1—dc21   2001002222

Printed in Singapore
Bound in the United States of America
1 2 3 4 5 6 – OS – 07 06 05 04 03 02

The authors are grateful to Katy Holmgren, whose excellent editing of the manuscript has made this book such a pleasure to read.

Front cover picture: *A painting shows a family returning to their battle-scarred home in Fredericksburg, Virginia.*

Back cover picture: *A family camps with an infantry regiment near Washington, D.C.*

Contents

WORDS YOU NEED TO KNOW

>‑+‑}‑+‑O‑+‑{‑+‑<

blockade: warships organized to keep all ships from delivering goods and supplies to an enemy harbor. During the Civil War, the North set up blockades of all Southern ports.

casualties: soldiers or civilians who are killed, wounded, captured by the enemy, or missing as a result of a battle

civilian: a person who is not in the military

Copperheads: the name for Northerners who were against the Civil War

draft: to require a person to join the military

economy: a system of producing, moving, buying and selling all the things a country needs

Emancipation Proclamation: a decree (order) issued by President Abraham Lincoln on September 22, 1862, to free all slaves in the Confederate states

home front: all of the people, activities, and places of a nation at war that are not part of the military

immigrants: people who move from one nation to another nation

inflation: a drop in the value of money, and a rise in prices caused by shortages of goods

manufacturing: making goods at a factory, using machines run by a large number of workers

morale: the confidence, courage, and fighting spirit of soldiers; also, the willingness of civilians to let their country keep fighting

occupation: enemy soldiers living in and controlling a town or area

plantation: a very large farm, with hundreds of acres, in the Southern United States. A plantation usually grew a single crop and had slaves to do the work. The owner of a plantation was called a planter.

prejudice: unreasonable hatred of a group of people

rebels: the nickname used by Northerners to refer to the citizens of the Southern states, who were in rebellion against the United States

recruit: to persuade men to join the army or navy

refugees: people who flee from their homes to escape danger, especially during times of war

siege: an effort to capture a place by surrounding it, shooting at it, and cutting it off from food and supplies

Yankees: the Southern nickname for the citizens of the Northern states

INTRODUCTION

A COUNTRY AT WAR

The Northern states and the Southern states had begun growing apart even before the American Revolution (1775–1783). Life in the North was very different from life in the South. The North and South disagreed about slavery. Southerners believed that slavery was right, and Northerners believed it was wrong. They also disagreed about whether the Southern states had the right to leave the United States of America.

In 1861 the Southern states formed their own nation, named the Confederate States of America, also called "the Confederacy." The Confederates believed that they had to fight the North to win their independence. Northerners called the United States "the Union." They wanted to keep both Northern and Southern states unified, or together, as one nation. Northerners were willing to fight to accomplish this goal to preserve the Union. So the Civil War began in 1861.

During the Civil War, life in the North differed greatly from life in the South. The war brought poverty and hunger to some of the people at home and enormous changes to daily life. Those who stayed home made the supplies that the Union and Confederate armies and navies needed to fight the war. They also had to carry on with day-to-day life while their husbands, fathers, brothers, and sons went to war.

CHAPTER ONE

The Northern Home Front

The North before the Civil War

At the beginning of the Civil War, about twenty million people lived in the North. Four million of them had arrived from Europe less than ten years before. Most of them came from Germany or Ireland. Three-quarters of these new arrivals, called immigrants, settled in Northern cities and got jobs in factories. The rest settled in the smaller towns and countryside of the North. About 200,000 free blacks lived in the North. Most of them lived in cities and worked at low-paying jobs.

The North had both farms and factories. Early in the nation's history, nine out of ten Americans had lived on farms. In the years between the American Revolution and the Civil War, many people in the Northern states moved to towns and cities to work in businesses and factories. By 1860 one-quarter of the Northern population lived in cities or large towns. Another quarter lived in small towns.

About one-half of all Northerners still lived on farms. Most farmers were not rich, but they were able to make a living. Farmers produced enough food to feed their own families and extra food to sell to people living in cities. The ability of Northern farms to grow food—wheat, corn, fruit, and vegetables—and to raise livestock made it possible for the North to feed both civilians and soldiers during the Civil War. They did this even with one in every three farmers gone to war.

The North led the United States in manufacturing. Newly invented machines, such

Northerners knew that farms were important to their well-being. A magazine shows an image of plenty.

as the sewing machine, allowed workers to produce large numbers of goods quickly. More rapid types of transportation—such as steamboats and steam-powered train engines—replaced sailing ships, flatboats, and horse-drawn wagons. It became possible to send the goods all over the country.

Factories were cold in winter and were hot and stuffy in the summer. If a factory worker got badly hurt by a machine, that was just part of the job. The owners of businesses and factories were often wealthy. Factory workers, both men and women, labored for as long as sixteen hours a day, six days a week. For this they got paid less than one dollar a day.

The poorest workers—especially women, children, and recent immigrants—worked long hours in poor conditions. Workers hoped to save enough money to buy farms or start their own businesses. But most could hardly afford enough food or a place to live. About one-half of the people in Northern cities and towns made a comfortable living. The other half struggled to make ends meet.

Factory workers, including a young boy, walk to their jobs. During the Civil War, some soldiers' children left school to take over their fathers' jobs.

Northern states offered free education to all children, rich or poor. But parents did not have to send their children to school. Only about one-half of Northern children attended school. Many parents were so poor that they needed the money that their children could make working at jobs. Laws allowed young children to work.

WHO JOINED THE UNION ARMY?

A total of about two million men served in the Union army during the Civil War. About half of these men were farmers (half the total Northern population were farmers). About 200,000 German immigrants served in the Union army, along with 150,000 Irish immigrants and 186,000 black men. Union soldiers came from all occupations and economic classes. Civil War army regiments elected their own officers. The wealthy and well-known men in each community were usually elected as officers. Working-class men entered the army as privates, the lowest rank.

Johnny Clem, above, *ran away from home to be a Union drummer boy when he was only ten years old. The Union army had about 40,000 drummer boys, and the Confederate army had 20,000. Clem stayed in the army until 1915 and eventually became a general. Young boys,* left, *also joined the navies during the Civil War. Boys who brought gunpowder to the gun crews during naval battles were called "powder monkeys."*

Children worked as many hours as adults but for less pay, because they couldn't work as fast. In 1860 more than 100,000 Northern children worked as servants. Another 100,000 worked in factories and mines. In one Northern factory, one worker in five was under age sixteen. Children as young as six worked in factories, doing such jobs as spinning thread, sewing garments, or assembling shoes. Some poor children who didn't work in factories sold newspapers and other items or shined shoes on city streets.

The North had an excellent system of transportation. Ships, wagons, and trains delivered goods and supplies throughout the North and to parts of the South controlled by the Union army. This photograph shows the harbor at City Point, Virginia, in 1864.

The Northern states had the people, the farms, and the factories they needed to produce plentiful food and manufactured goods. Then came the Civil War. Thousands of Northern men between the ages of eighteen and forty-five marched off to fight. By the end of the war, one-half of the men in this age group—about two million in all—would join the Union army.

The North at War

When the Civil War began, Northern factories bought more machines and hired people to work longer hours. Factories would supply all the needs of the home front and produce everything that the military needed to fight the war— uniforms, underwear, boots and shoes, hats, blankets, tents, swords, pistols, muskets, cannons, ammunition, wagons, lumber, shovels, steamboats, and surgical instruments. Machine shops, factories, and gunpowder mills in the

In a New York factory, workers pour hot metal into a mold to make a Union cannon.

North all supplied the military. And most importantly, throughout the war, the North's system of roads, rivers, canals, and railroads worked well to move the supplies to where they were needed.

Before the Civil War, many Northern businesses had bought Southern cotton and sold goods to Southern customers. Northern banks had loaned large sums of money to Southern borrowers. When the war began, businesses lost their Southern customers. Banks could not collect the money owed them by Southern borrowers. This drove many Northerners out of business. Those who managed to stay in business soon made a lot of money producing and selling supplies and weapons to the U.S. government.

The U.S. government spent one to two million dollars a day during the war to supply the army and navy. To help the North pay for the war, the U.S. government printed paper money. Congress passed a law making paper money just as valuable as gold or silver coins. Congress also passed laws creating new taxes so the Union could collect money for the war. For the first time in U.S. history, the federal government taxed people's income. It also taxed tobacco, liquor, and the sale of most consumer goods, such as carriages, jewelry, meats, and medicines.

The North had some problems producing military supplies. The manufacturers tried to produce so many goods so quickly that some did a very poor job. People began to use a new word, "shoddy," to describe woolen uniforms and blankets that tore or fell apart soon after being given to soldiers. Soldiers soon began to use "shoddy" to describe all sorts of badly made things: uniforms that wore out quickly, cartridge boxes that fell apart in the first rain, or wooden items that twisted and warped because they were made from green lumber.

Some business owners tried to make money in dishonest ways. They charged the army high prices for poorly made or worn-out supplies. Buyers and sellers, called "speculators," collected large amounts of useful materials, such as shoe leather. Then they kept the supplies and waited for the price to rise. When the price went up high enough, they sold the supplies to become rich. A New York newspaper wrote in

Women at work preparing ammunition at the U.S. Arsenal in Watertown, Massachusetts

1863 about the methods of one speculator: "Mr. A. T. Stewart of this city . . . has been . . . buying up all the goods he could purchase. . . . Warehouses [have been] rented and filled to the rafters with goods, and, this done . . . he closed sales and waited for coming events. It is well known that Mr. Stewart's connection with the government is such that he has early information of changes to take place. . . . "

Some Northern merchants sent goods to foreign ports such as Bermuda. They sold the goods to men who owned blockade-runners, fast ships that ran through the Union blockade into Confederate ports. In this way, they hid what they were doing. But they were really selling supplies to the enemy and helping Confederate forces to fight and kill Union soldiers.

For most people on the home front, making a living during the Civil War became harder. Businesses that produced and sold food and other essential goods raised prices. They were able to do this because the military needed everything the factories could make and would pay any price. Yet wages did not go up as quickly for the people who produced the goods, because there were still plenty of workers. Even though thousands of men went to war, women, immigrants, and freed slaves took their places in the factories. So business owners made a lot of money, while workers had to struggle to buy what they needed.

When prices go up because there are not enough important goods to go around, this is called inflation. When a nation's economy has inflation, the value of money goes down. It takes more money to buy the same goods. For example, in the North, between · 1861 and 1863, wages doubled, and the price of coffee quadrupled.

Some women made a living during the Civil War by becoming sutlers, who sold food, drink, and other supplies to soldiers.

The Union army promised to pay its soldiers about thirteen dollars a month. The soldiers' pay did not make up for the money the soldiers had made at home or for the work they had done on their farms. Often the pay arrived late. And more time passed as the soldiers sent their pay home to their families.

Women and children had to get jobs to make up for the money their soldier husbands and fathers had made. Some worked in factories, while others took in sewing or rented out rooms. About 100,000 Northern women went to work at factories during the war. One of every three wartime factory workers in the North was a woman.

Women and children also did the farming work of absent fathers, brothers, and sons. An Iowa woman wrote to her soldier husband, "We have got our garden plowed and planted . . . Lib and I planted the corn & potatoes ourselves. We didn't know where to find anybody to do it for us so pitched in and planted it ourselves." A magazine reported, "We have seen . . . a stout matron whose sons are in the army, with her team cutting hay . . . and she cut seven acres with ease in a day."

Most of the folk back home took on extra work without complaining. A mother on a farm in Rhode Island wrote to her soldier son, "We have no extra help...Father has done your part of the work." An Iowa woman wrote, "our hired man left to enlist just as corn planting [began], so I shouldered my hoe and have worked out ever since." A wife in Massachusetts wrote her husband, "Emma [their daughter] is so large now she helps considerable.... My wood is all saved up...and I have got it paid...so you see I am getting along pretty well."

Sometimes hard work was not enough. When the father and brothers of a Michigan frontier family joined the army, a girl and her mother rented out rooms in their house, sold quilts, took in sewing, and taught school. Still, they had to struggle "to keep our land, pay our taxes, and to live." A farmer's wife in Illinois wrote to her soldier husband, "For God sake do come home. I am sick. There is nothing in the house to live on.... The cows got in, and ate up the garden, and everything has gone to the devil and you just have to come."

A woman in a textile (cloth) mill threads a loom for weaving cloth.

Chapter Two

The Southern Home Front

The South before the Civil War

Before the Civil War, about nine million people lived in the South. About three and one-half million of them were slaves. The South also had about 135,000 free blacks, whose ancestors had been freed by their owners.

In the South, wealthy white people owned black people and forced them to work. Many white people in the South thought black people were not quite human. The owners, or masters, had the power of life and death over their slaves. An owner could beat, or even kill, a slave and not be punished for it. It was against the law to teach a black person to read and write. And an owner could, and often did, split up slaves' families by selling husbands, wives, and children to different owners in far-off states. When this happened, the slaves almost never saw their families again.

About one-half of Southern whites made up a middle class of small farmers. One-half were poor and struggling, and a very small portion was made up of wealthy planters. The people who owned large numbers of slaves had money and political power. They passed laws that favored their way of life. One white Southern household out of four owned slaves. One-half of these owned fewer than five slaves. Those Southern whites who didn't own slaves hoped to one day make enough money to buy some. In the South, white people saw slaves as possessions like fine houses and clothes, which made a person seem wealthy and important.

Wealthy Southern planters lived on large farms called plantations. On the plantations, slaves did the work of planting and harvesting cotton, the South's main crop. Here, a wealthy family at home enjoy a game of croquet on the lawn of their plantation house.

THE LIFE OF A SLAVE

Slave owners controlled every part of their slaves' lives. Some owners made their slaves work so hard that when they weren't working all they could do was sleep. Most slaves woke up before sunrise and started planting or harvesting as soon as it was light enough to see. They worked in the fields until dark. Women with newborn babies carried them to the fields. After dark, slaves sat up for several hours spinning thread, weaving cloth, and making clothing. Slaves who worked in the owner's house had easier lives. They cooked and served meals, did laundry, cleaned house, polished silver, helped their owners get dressed, and even fanned flies away from their faces. Slaves also hauled water from the well, cut firewood, took care of the horses, and did any other job that had to be done.

Slaves lived in small, one-room log cabins around their owners' mansions. They slept on mattresses filled with cornhusks. Some owners let their slaves have small garden plots to grow vegetables for themselves. Each slave was allowed a couple of new pieces of clothing and a pair of shoes each year.

Slave owners could break up slaves'

families at any time. For this reason, owners did not allow slaves to have legal or religious weddings. But they did want slaves to have children, because the children became the owners' property. So owners held a marriage ceremony in which the

Household slaves sweep a courtyard.

slave couple jumped over a broom. After that, the couple lived together.

If their owners permitted it, slaves held dances on Saturday nights and went to church on Sundays. Where owners did not allow slaves to pray together, slaves sometimes held secret prayer meetings. Many free blacks and slaves became ministers and led groups of black people in prayer. Others were excellent singers or musicians who played at dances. Slaves often made up songs and sang together while working in the fields. But some owners did not allow singing. A former Alabama slave explained, "They tried to make them stop singing and praying . . . because all they'd ask for was to be set free, but the slaves would get in the cabins and turn a big wash pot upside down and sing into that, and the noise couldn't get out."

Some slaves were allowed to visit slaves on other plantations. They had to carry passes to show to any patrollers they met. At night, patrollers with dogs looked for slaves who had left their plantations without passes. As slaves were sold from one plantation to another, they talked with one another and learned about the cruelty or kindness of different owners.

Before the Civil War, the Southern states accounted for only 18 percent of the total manufacturing in the United States. Massachusetts alone produced manufactured goods worth 50 percent more than those produced in the entire South. The Southern economy and way of life were based almost entirely on agriculture (farming). Most white Southern workers believed that farming was a better way of life and had no wish to work in a factory. Wealthy white men preferred to buy land and slaves rather than open a factory. Fewer than 10 percent of all Southerners lived in a town. New Orleans, Louisiana—the Confederacy's largest city—had a population of about 168,000. In contrast, New York City had one million people.

Southern agriculture depended heavily on cotton and slaves. The slaves did the work of growing and harvesting the cotton. Planters sold the cotton to factories in the North and in Europe. Factory workers used machines to spin the cotton into thread and weave the thread into cloth. With the money earned from the sale of cotton, Southern plantation owners bought most of what they needed to live—food, clothing, furniture, farming tools—from the Northern states and from Europe. Southern planters had no need for factories as long as they could buy what they needed with the profits of selling cotton.

Wealthy planters lived in mansions on huge plantations with hundreds of slaves. The planters were only a tiny percentage of the total Southern population—one-half of 1 percent, about 45,000 people. Plantations grew huge fields of a single crop. Most raised cotton, but some planters grew tobacco, rice, or sugar. Planters' wives and daughters supervised the house slaves, gave medicines to the sick, and read the Bible to their

Slaves in South Carolina return from the fields carrying loads of freshly picked cotton.

slaves on Sunday mornings. But much of the time they lived lives of leisure and culture, visiting with friends, reading, or playing the piano.

About one-half of the white Southern population had farms of 100 acres or less, which they worked themselves. They grew some cotton and mostly raised food for their own families.

The South also had about two million "poor whites," who lived on land with poor soil and just barely got by with hunting and fishing. Southern white women in the non-slave-owning classes did the hard work of farming and housekeeping. Most of these women did not have jobs outside their homes and farms.

About one-third of Southern white children received an education. Only four Southern states had public school systems. Planters' children received a few years of private tutoring. The sons attended schools in the northeast or in Europe. Daughters received lessons at home. Middle-class and poor white children attended schools only if they lived near one and their parents didn't need them to work. Some parents taught their own children to read, write, and do sums.

Slave children did not attend school. A small number of owners broke the law and secretly taught their slaves to read and write. The slaves in turn taught other slaves. Many owners punished slaves if they caught them with books or pencils. Free blacks could not attend white public schools, so they started their own schools. Some of these schools were wrecked by mobs of white people who did not want to see blacks improve themselves.

The South had 9,000 miles of railroad track when the Civil War began. This was not very much track to cover such a large area. Not all of the track was the same width. Some sections of track did not meet up with any other tracks. Workers unloaded goods from one train and moved them by wagon to another train miles away. The Southern railroads filled the needs of the prewar South, but they would not be enough for a country at war.

War Comes to the South

The Civil War brought three major changes to life in the South. First, most of the South's able-bodied white men left their homes to fight for the Confederacy. About one million men joined the Confederate military during the Civil War. This was 80 to 90 percent of the South's able-bodied

WHO JOINED THE CONFEDERATE ARMY?

About one million Confederate men fought in the Civil War. Wealthy men—planters or planters' sons—were elected as army officers. Only one-quarter of the common soldiers came from families who owned slaves. Three-quarters of the Confederate soldiers were either planters or farmers. A large number of them, possibly one-half, couldn't read or write. They had to have other soldiers read their letters to them and write out their answers. One soldier proudly wrote to his mother, "Maw I have lurned to write in Camp well a nuf to write my leters my self." The South was more rural than the North. Many Southern soldiers already knew how to ride horses and handle guns. Northern soldiers had to be taught to ride.

white men. The Confederate military also took about 40,000 slaves away from plantations to use as laborers and servants. The people left behind struggled to feed their families and to supply food to the Confederate army. Second, the Union navy's blockade of Southern seaports prevented trading ships from exporting cotton and bringing in food, clothing, and other goods. Finally, most of the Civil War's battles took place in the South. Bloody fighting and destruction came to Southern towns and farms.

The city of Charleston, South Carolina, in ruins, 1865

Slave owners used cruel methods to try to stop their slaves from running away.

The civilians on the home front took on new and different kinds of jobs, including many they had never done before. For example, in January 1863, a Confederate general, once a planter, wrote to his wife "you must be housekeeper, overseer, man of all business, and everything." As the Union blockade took effect, most planters stopped growing cotton and began growing food and raising livestock. Their wives and daughters learned about such tasks as growing food crops, spinning, weaving, making salt to preserve meat, and supervising the slaves who did these jobs. When their men went off to war, planters' families did not endure as much hardship as non-slave-owning families, because they had slaves to do all the work.

Slave owners feared that slaves would try to escape when they heard about the war. Some owners put their slaves in chains to keep them from running away. Owners tried to track down runaway slaves with dogs. When they found runaway slaves, they punished them, usually by whipping. Other owners sold the captured slaves away from their families.

A former Alabama slave described how the "overseer begun to drive us around like . . . cattle. Every time they would hear the Yankees was coming they would take us out in the woods and hide us. Finally they sold us after carrying us away from Bolivar County. Some of us was sold to people in Demopolis, Alabama, and Atlanta, Georgia, and some to folks in . . . Mississippi. I don't anymore know where my own folks went to than you do."

The wives and children of owners of small farms already knew how to raise food crops. Still, without the men around, they had much extra work. The work became harder after the Confederate government set a new tax that required both rich planters and poor farmers to give 10 percent of all the food they produced to the army.

The farms and plantations grew enough food to feed everyone. As the war went on, the food became more difficult to transport. First, the food had to be hauled in wagons to the nearest railroad. But the Confederate army needed many of the South's horses and mules. Few animals were left to haul the wagons. When farm wagons broke, they could not be fixed, because the men who fixed wagons were in the army. Also, the army used most of the material needed to repair wagons.

During the war, the South's railroads and engines wore out. There were too few parts to fix them. Also, when the Union army advanced into the South, soldiers tore up the tracks, stuck the rails in huge bonfires, and twisted the red-hot metal around tree trunks so that it could never be used again. Because of the South's transportation problems, food spoiled in the countryside. City dwellers and soldiers went hungry.

The Union naval blockade also changed life in the South. In 1860, the year before the war began, about 6,000 ships had entered Southern ports. They delivered all the things produced by the manufacturing world: railroad engines and parts to repair engines, iron to build wagons, and machines to harvest food. The blockade gradually cut off the South from the manufacturing world. At the beginning of the Civil War, the blockade stopped one ship in ten from entering Southern ports. By 1864 the Union navy caught one ship in three.

Only a few hundred ships, called blockade-runners, entered Southern ports each year during the war. Most blockade-runners delivered important war supplies such as guns and ammunition, leather, medical supplies, and clothing. The blockade forced the South to build factories or to expand the ones it already had.

The blockade prevented the South's factories from getting raw materials to keep producing. Even so, the Southerners built textile mills to make cloth for uniforms, armories to make guns, and shipyards to make ships. The Tredegar Iron Works at Richmond, Virginia—the largest factory in the South—had 2,500 workers in 1863. Tredegar made locomotives, cannons, ammunition, and armor plating for ships.

Factories needed workers. Because most men were off to war, thousands of Southern women who had never before held jobs went to work. In

Richmond, the Confederate government hired more than 2,000 women to sew uniforms. Another 3,000 worked on uniforms in Atlanta, Georgia. Thousands more women throughout the Confederacy made uniforms, shoes, and blankets for the army. They earned about two Confederate dollars a day. About 500 women worked at Confederate ammunition factories. They did the dangerous work of filling shells with explosive powder. Two explosions took place at Southern ammunition factories during the war. Forty-five women and girls were killed.

By building its own factories, the Confederacy increased its ability to manufacture supplies for the war. The army and the civilian population still ran out of many things. So, Southerners figured out ways to make do. Unable to get lamp oil from the North, they used homemade candles. Lacking leather, they made shoes from wood or cloth. They made toothbrushes out of twigs, carved combs out of wood, and gathered plants to use as medicines.

Tredegar Iron Works in Richmond, Virginia, was the most important iron factory in the South.

Life Gets Harder

Like the government in the North, the Confederate government tried to make up for the wartime shortage of gold and silver coins by printing a large amount of paper money. The Confederate government promised to give people gold or silver coins in exchange for the paper money—after they won the war. So, Southerners didn't trust their paper money. This lack of trust caused people to set very high prices on things they wanted to sell. At the same time, wages went up, but not nearly as high as prices.

The Confederate army set soldiers' pay at eleven dollars a month (in Confederate dollars). The Confederate army often let months go by without paying the soldiers. When a Confederate soldier got captured, he received no pay at all for the time he spent in a Union prison. Soldiers' families suffered as a result.

RISING PRICES AND WAGES IN THE CONFEDERACY

	1861	1863
Machinists at Tredegar	$5/day	$10/day
Munitions workers (Female)	$4/week	$6/day
Beef	$1/pound	$8
Butter	$3	$15–20
Flour	$8/barrel	$30
Shoes	$25/pair	$500
Monthly food bill for the family	$6.65	$68

Like the North, the South had speculators. Some men in charge of collecting food and supplies for the Confederate army sold them at high prices instead of passing them on to the soldiers. Southern newspapers expressed people's anger at such actions. They called speculators "vampires" who "would bottle the . . . air and sell it at so much a bottle," while "our brave soldiers are off battling the [North]."

All of these problems made Southern life harder. One Mississippi family had a variety of food and plenty to eat in 1862. A year later, the family had only rice, milk, and cornbread to eat. The only meat they could get came from rats and mules. In 1863 one person wrote, "rats are a luxury." In April 1863, a Richmond woman led hundreds of women and men into the city's streets. Angry about food shortages and high prices, they broke windows to steal food from shops. They did not stop until Confederate president Jefferson Davis himself arrived, then threatened to have soldiers shoot at them.

A Richmond man with a high-paying job still could not afford enough food to keep himself and his family from hunger. He wrote in his diary in 1864, "I cannot afford to have more than an ounce of meat daily for each member of my family. . . . This is famine [severe shortage of food]." A ten-year-old Atlanta girl wrote in 1864, "The times are getting a little worse every day. I will have to go to work to help Mama."

A War-Torn Country
Only two major battles took place in Northern states: Antietam in Maryland and Gettysburg in Pennsylvania. The rebel (Confederate) army retreated south after both battles. The Civil War brought the Union army down the rivers and across state lines into Confederate territory. The

An abandoned plantation house, right, *occupied by Union troops in South Carolina*

A family of refugees, below, *with their belongings piled on a cart. Hundreds of refugees from surrounding areas crowded into Southern cities, where often an entire family had to share a rented room. Food became scarce. In 1864 a girl in Atlanta, Georgia, wrote on her tenth birthday, "I did not have a cake times were too hard so I celebrated with ironing."*

Union took over Southern ports, including New Orleans. Major battles raged in Virginia, Tennessee, Mississippi, Georgia, and other Confederate states. With each passing year of the war, the Union army occupied more of the South.

Soldiers from both armies took food from Southern farms and plantations. Later in the war, Union soldiers had orders to destroy everything they couldn't take. They burned barns, killed farm animals, and urged the slaves to escape. The Union believed that by destroying or taking property and freeing slaves, they would starve the rebels and make them give up fighting.

A UNION OFFICER'S LETTER, MAY 1863

I burned all [food], produce [wheat and corn], and forage [hay], all mills and tan-yards, and destroyed everything that would in any way aid the enemy. . . . I also destroyed telegraph and railroad between Tuscumbia and Decatur [Alabama], and all the [boats] between Savannah (Tennessee) and Courtland [Alabama]. . . . [The expedition] has [ruined] one of the best [wheat and corn growing areas] of the South, preventing them from raising another crop this year, and taking away from them some 1,500 negroes.

We found large quantities of shelled corn, all ready for shipment, also bacon, and gave it to the flames.

A group of soldiers return to camp with geese and a hog taken from their owner.

Thousands of Southern farmers who lived close to the fighting fled to towns and cities. Food became scarcer as fewer people worked the farms. A man looking back on his Southern Civil War childhood wrote, "starvation is one of the sharpest memories of my childhood . . . by the time I was seven or eight years old, I had to work almost like a man, helping mother to keep life in myself and my younger sisters and brothers."

But even in cities, Confederate civilians could not escape the war. When Union artillery shot at Southern cities, people stayed in their basements

Refugees fleeing from the bombardment of Charleston, South Carolina, in 1863. During the Civil War, about 250,000 Southerners fled their homes. A Georgia girl wrote in her diary, "Papa says he don't know where on earth to go."

during the worst of the attacks. The rest of the time, people tried to live normal lives. A ten-year-old Atlanta girl wrote in 1864, "I knit all the morning. In the evening we had to run to Auntie's to get in the cellar."

The Union Army and the Slaves

When the Union army was far away, most slaves stayed on the plantations. They kept working for their owners. Many slaves had not heard about the Emancipation Proclamation and did not know that the Union wanted to set them free. They did not learn about freedom until the Union army arrived.

Former slaves from Alabama later explained: "Us heard talk about the war, but us didn't pay no attention. Us never dreamed that freedom would ever come." "We work right on 'till one day somebody sent a runner saying the Yankees coming. . . . Weren't long after that they tell us we'se free." "When we heard dat us was free [we all] marched to [town] and had a celebration."

A Mississippi planter reported in 1863, "When the advanced forces of the enemy [the Yankees] reached [us] . . . the hoe and plow handle dropped from the hands of the Negroes, and I ceased to be a planter forever."

A Union soldier wrote to his brother from North Carolina in 1865, "I have talked with many of the colored people of NC. . . . They knew full well what our army signified to them . . . they hid away from the fleeing rebels, but all turned out to welcome us . . . jumping & dancing along the street & shouting 'I'se broke my chain; I'se broke my chain.'"

More than 500,000 slaves escaped when the fighting brought the Union army close to their homes. At least 100,000 then joined the Union army, and another 100,000 worked as laborers for the army. When the slaves escaped, slave owners had to do their own work for the first time in their lives.

President Abraham Lincoln issued the Emancipation Proclamation in 1862 to free all the slaves in the Confederate states. When one slave heard about the proclamation, he spoke for many when he said that "Abe Lincoln was the best president that this country ever had. If it hadn't been for him we'd still be slaves right now."

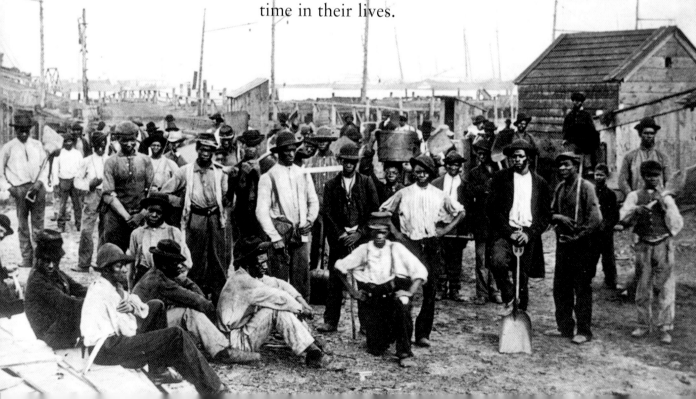

CHAPTER THREE

The Hearts and Minds of the People

Most people supported the Civil War when it began. Both Northerners and Southerners believed that the war would be short and glorious. People in both the North and the South believed that they were in the right and would easily win the war. Families on both sides saw all their male members rush to become soldiers in the first weeks of the war. For example, seven Virginia brothers enlisted in a Confederate regiment. A Union family in Iowa saw six brothers and their father off to war, while the mother went to work as a nurse. A Confederate soldier described how his mother "had buckled on his armor, and told him to go and battle for his country." Such scenes were repeated in homes throughout the North and the South.

Women saw the soldiers off with words of encouragement. Thousands of civilians showed their support for the war by volunteering to help. They made uniforms and bandages for soldiers and worked in hospitals caring for wounded soldiers.

As soldiers died and food became expensive and difficult to get, growing numbers of people on both sides began to turn against the war. They began to question whether it was worth fighting, dying, or starving for the Union or the Confederacy.

Divided Families

The Civil War has been called a war in which brother fought against brother. In other words, families could split apart, with some men fighting

for the North and some fighting for the South. The war divided the families of low-ranking privates and the families of high-ranking generals.

During the Siege of Vicksburg in the summer of 1863, Missouri soldiers fought for each side. One

Southern women sew for Confederate soldiers.

night a rebel soldier called out to the Union camp to ask if there were any Missouri men in the Union lines. A Union soldier said, "yes."

The rebel soldier asked, "Is Tom Jones there?"

A Union soldier answered, "He is. Is that you, Jim?"

It was. The brothers met. The Confederate soldier Jim gave his brother Tom money to send to the folks back home.

John C. Pemberton was a professional soldier who had been born in Pennsylvania. In April 1861, when the war was just beginning, Pemberton's two brothers joined the Philadelphia City Troop in the United States cavalry. His mother wondered why John did not return home and do the same.

But Pemberton had married a Virginia woman who wrote him a letter at this time, "My darling husband, why are you not with us? Why do you stay [in the North]? Jeff Davis [the Confederate president] has a post ready for you." Pemberton thought about what his mother and brothers wanted him to do. He thought about what his wife wanted him to do. It was a painful decision, but John C. Pemberton joined the Confederate army. He could not fight for the North while his wife remained loyal to the South.

Usually, families that split apart when the war began did not get back together until the war ended. However, both the Union and Confederate armies let women and children travel from one side to the other. So sometimes, divided families could visit.

For example, Confederate colonel William Lamb commanded Fort Fisher near Wilmington, North Carolina. Before the war, Lamb had traveled to Providence, Rhode Island. He met and married Sarah Anne Chafee, called Daisy. When

A Union family do chores together in a camp near Washington, D.C.

the war began, William sent Daisy and their three small children to live with his family in Norfolk, Virginia. Then, in 1862, the Yankees captured Norfolk. Daisy and the children went north to her family in Rhode Island.

Daisy missed her husband. She and her parents persuaded Union officials to let her and her two oldest children travel to the South. Daisy joined her husband in 1863 at Fort Fisher, where battles were not taking place. When William was not on duty, the family ate and played together. They took the children for walks on the beach. At night they read aloud to their children.

Later, in 1865, Union soldiers and sailors attacked Fort Fisher. Daisy and the children watched with fear. They were lucky because William Lamb survived the battle, although he was seriously wounded.

The Lamb family was unusual. Most Union and Confederate soldiers often did not have a chance to see their families. Families stayed in touch by writing letters. More than 100,000 letters a day passed between Union soldiers and their families during the war. Good news from home helped keep soldiers' spirits up. But bad news worried them, especially because the soldiers knew that they could not help their families.

A New York soldier wrote, "Dear Father, Mother, and Sister: As yet I have no mail and am living in great [worry]. I see by the papers that there has been very high water nearly all over the state. Therefore you must have had your share but I hope you are all safe."

Families were lucky if their soldiers got home once a year for a visit. One Confederate soldier who managed to get home was Wesley Culp.

Culp was born and lived on a hill just outside of Gettysburg, Pennsylvania. When the war began, Wesley left his family to join the Confederate army in Virginia. In the summer of 1863, Wesley was happy because his army was marching into Pennsylvania.

A big battle took place around his hometown. Wesley's unit received orders to charge some Union soldiers defending the top of a hill. Wesley Culp was killed during the charge. He fell on Culp's Hill, the hill where his family lived.

Home Front Volunteers

Thousands of people wanted to help soldiers out of patriotism and love for their fathers, husbands, sons, and brothers. On both the Northern and the Southern home fronts, people formed volunteer aid societies to help their soldiers. They collected food and organized special fairs to raise money. The fairs charged admission fees and sold snacks and crafts. Children held their own fund-raisers, such as snack stands, at these fairs. In the South, the Women's Relief Society of the Confederate States held concerts to raise money for medical supplies. Northern aid societies run by women collected about fifty million dollars of contributions to the Union cause.

Ladies' aid societies formed sewing circles in many towns. Women and children gathered at people's homes to make uniforms, socks, underwear, blankets, and bandages to send to their hometown soldiers. Members read soldiers' letters to the group to share news about the war.

Women sent soldiers packages of homemade food and clothing containing encouraging notes to the strangers who would receive them. One woman wrote, "My dear Friend, You are not my husband nor son; but you are the husband or son of some woman who undoubtedly loves you as I love mine. I have made these garments for you with a heart that aches for your sufferings."

The largest and most important volunteer aid society in the North was the U.S. Sanitary Commission. Founded in 1861, it operated throughout the nation. The commission worked for better living conditions in army camps and better medical care for soldiers.

Army camps were cold, wet, and filthy places. Soldiers got sick and died just from living in the camps. In the winter, bad weather made soldiers sick. In warmer weather, mosquitoes, which were common in the South, spread serious illnesses such as malaria.

The Sanitary Commission organized the shipment of food, medical supplies, clothing, and blankets to Union army camps. The commission also set up lodges near railroad stations where soldiers on their way home could stay. The commission made up a list of soldiers who were in hospitals so their families could keep track of them. It provided free lodging for family members who traveled to visit soldiers in hospitals. Commission workers gave out water and hot soup to wounded soldiers after battles.

Members of a Union volunteer group called the Christian Commission distribute donated supplies to soldiers in 1862. The commission helped and fed wounded soldiers, conducted religious services at army camps, and distributed donated food, clothing, and Bibles and other books to soldiers.

The South did not have a nation-wide group to aid soldiers, but many towns and cities set up local aid societies. They collected donations of food, clothing, and blankets and sent them to Confederate soldiers.

More than 3,000 women on each side volunteered to work as nurses and to take care of wounded soldiers. They worked in field hospitals near the battlefields and in permanent hospitals in cities such as Washington, D.C., and Richmond, Virginia. Nurses washed and bandaged wounds, gave the patients food and medicine, wrote

Hundreds of nuns, like this Sister of Mercy, above left, *served as volunteer nurses during the Civil War.*

Clara Barton, above right, *organized a nursing and supply service for the Union army, collected money to buy medical supplies, and delivered them to the battlefields. Barton saw many terrible things as she worked. After a battle in Virginia, she saw 3,000 wounded soldiers who had to lie on the ground with only hay under them while they waited to be taken by train to a hospital. One time, while she tried to help a wounded soldier, a bullet passed through her sleeve and killed the soldier. Soldiers called her "the angel of the battlefield."*

letters to patients' families, and comforted dying men. Most of these women had no experience as nurses and had to learn on the job. One woman wrote, "The foul air from this mass of human beings at first made me giddy and sick, but I soon got over it. We have to walk and when we give the men anything kneel in blood and water; but we think nothing of it."

Dr. Mary Edwards Walker, left, *was only twenty years old when the Civil War began. She spent the first three years of the war working as a nurse. She later worked as an assistant surgeon for an Ohio regiment in the Union army. She was the first woman to hold such a job. Dr. Walker received the Congressional Medal of Honor after the war in 1866. She was the first woman to receive this medal.*

Anne Bell, below, *was the matron, or nurse in charge, of a Union hospital in Tennessee.*

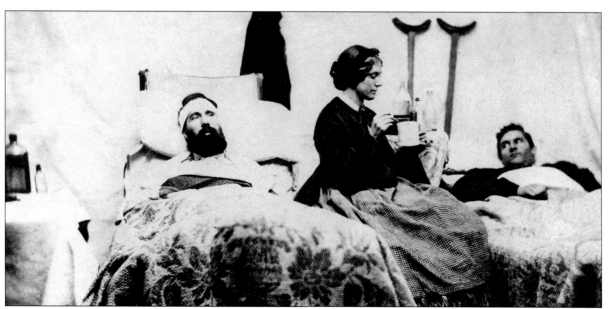

This Virginia house was used as a hospital after a battle. Wounded soldiers were taken to any available building— churches, hotels, warehouses, shops, barns, and homes.

Especially in the South, many doctors believed that women were too delicate for the work. But Southern women went to work in hospitals anyway. Their help was desperately needed. Men also volunteered to work as nurses. So many battles happened in the South that women near the battlefields took the wounded soldiers into their homes and cared for them.

Turning against the War

In the North, many people first supported the Civil War because it was a fight to save the Union. For example, in 1861 a Rhode Island soldier wrote to his children, "My life here, is not very pleasant, but I submit to it because I think it is for the best and it is the duty of us all, to do

Eliza Crim lived near the site of the Battle of New Market (May 1864). After the battle, she took in and cared for wounded soldiers.

what we can for our country and to preserve [the Union]. . . . It was given to us entire, and we must give it to you, entire."

Northerners began to turn against the war with the Emancipation Proclamation of September 1862. Abolitionists (the people working to abolish, or end, slavery) rejoiced. An Iowa father wrote to his soldier son that now the war is "God's war, and the object is to abolish slavery . . . and to [give] the black man . . . his natural and [lawful] rights."

Some Northern people believed that the war should only be about restoring the Union, not about ending slavery. Antiwar groups spread throughout the North. They carried banners that said things like "The Constitution As It Is, The Union As It Was" and "We won't fight to free [black people]." A Union soldier from Vermont wrote that "The boys think it is their duty to put down rebellion and nothing more, and they view the abolition of slavery in the present time as saddling so much additional labor upon them. . . . Negro prejudice is as strong here as anywhere."

Some Union soldiers overcame their prejudice against blacks because they saw how badly slave owners in the South treated slaves. They also saw how bravely black soldiers behaved in battles. Then they wrote letters to their families about what they had seen. One Rhode Island soldier wrote after a battle, "The 54th Mass[achusetts] Infantry 'colored' is as good a fighting regiment as there is. . . ." Over time, the number of Northerners who did not support emancipation of the slaves grew smaller.

The Draft

When the war began in 1861, the Union and Confederate armies easily filled their army units with eager volunteers. Many men volunteered because they were patriots. They believed that they should serve their country. Others volunteered for the adventure or for experience. The battles of

1861 and 1862 showed people that war was deadly. As a result, far fewer men volunteered.

The South realized that it had to do something to keep the armies full of men. In April 1862, the Confederate Congress passed the first draft law (also called a conscription law) in American history. All white males between eighteen and thirty-five years old who were not legally exempt (excused from having to serve) had to serve in the army for three years.

This draft favored rich men and slave owners. The law allowed one man to avoid being drafted for every twenty slaves owned by a family. For example, a family who owned forty slaves could keep both the father and son out of the army. The

Soldiers of Company E, 4th U.S. Colored Infantry at Fort Lincoln, Washington, D.C.

This cartoon from an 1862 New York newspaper makes fun of men who tried to avoid joining the army. Men tried many things, such as injuring themselves (as shown), pretending to be sick or insane, trying to bribe officials, fleeing to the West, or not showing up for service.

law also allowed any man to hire a substitute to serve in his place. Rich men hired poor men to go into the army for them. One Virginia planter even offered a farm to any man who would substitute for him.

Many Southerners disagreed with the draft because rich men could avoid it. They said that the war helped the rich, but that only the poor had to fight. The great majority of Southerners did not own slaves. They began to believe that the war had little to do with them. A struggling farmer's wife in North Carolina expressed the views of many when she wrote to the state governor, "I would like to know what he is fighting for. I don't think he is fighting for anything only for his family to starve."

The battles of 1862 showed the Confederate Congress that the first conscription law did not replace the armies' losses. So, in September 1862, Congress raised the draft age to forty-five. In February 1864, Congress changed the law so that white men between the ages of seventeen and fifty had to serve. Tens of thousands of drafted men never showed up for the army. Every time the South lost a battle, more soldiers deserted (or ran away from) the Confederate army. Many worried about their starving families at home. Most no longer believed in the war. During the Civil War, about 100,000 Confederate soldiers deserted the army. Many found Southern civilians who helped them hide. Several organized groups of deserters hid in the mountains and attacked Confederate soldiers who were trying to catch them.

The North had four times more white men of military age than the South. For this reason, the North waited longer before starting a draft. At the beginning of the war, the Union government

In New York, the Union army offered money to try to tempt poor immigrants to join.

asked soldiers to sign up for only three months. Before that time was up, the government began calling for three-year enlistments. Men did not want to be in the army for that long. By November 1862, the Northern states found that they could not raise enough volunteers for the Union army.

Several states, including Pennsylvania, Ohio, Indiana, and Wisconsin, tried a special draft to recruit soldiers. Angry mobs gathered to protest. In Indiana, the mob murdered two recruitment officers. Union soldiers had to restore order.

The U.S. Congress passed the Enrollment Act of March 3, 1863. All white men, whether single or married, between the ages of twenty and thirty-five, and all unmarried white men between the ages of thirty-five and forty-five, had to enter the draft. The Northern draft worked like a lottery, with names chosen by chance. The Enrollment Act let a man pay another man to serve as a substitute. Men could also avoid serving in the army by paying three hundred dollars to the government.

Draft lotteries were supposed to be fair. A Northern newspaper wrote in 1862 that the draft should "spare neither high nor low, rich nor poor, but reach all alike." However, there were several ways for wealthy men to avoid joining the army.

In the first Northern draft, 292,441 names were drawn. Only 9,881 men actually served. Most of the rest paid money to avoid serving. Poor whites were angry. They felt the law was unfair. The Enrollment Act led to draft riots.

The most famous riot took place in New York City in 1863. In New York, the draft began on July 11, 1863. An official drew the first names of the men who had to join the army. Newspapers published the names the next day. That afternoon the mobs started gathering. On July 13, more names were drawn and the rioting started. The mayor and the police could not restore order. As many as 50,000 people stormed through the streets. They burned a black church and orphanage. Rioting spread until large parts of New York were out of control. Rioters, mainly poor immigrant working men, made blacks their special victims. They brutally murdered about eleven blacks.

A New York woman described in her diary

The governor of New York asked President Lincoln to end the draft in order to end the rioting. This cartoon from 1863 makes fun of the governor, who is pretending to be strong. The original caption had the governor saying, "I have ordered the president to stop the draft!" In fact, the governor didn't order Lincoln to do anything, and Lincoln was not influenced by the governor's plea.

what took place, "Many were killed, many houses were gutted and burned: the colored [orphan] asylum was burned and all the furniture carried off by women: Negroes were hung in the street! . . . The laboring classes say they are sold for 300 dollars. . . ."

The violence in New York lasted four days. Soldiers from the Union army rushed to New York City. They put down the

riot by using their weapons. The soldiers killed or wounded more than one thousand rioters.

Even though the draft was unfair and unpopular, it continued. The draft in the North supplied enough men for the Union armies to continue to fight the war from 1863 until it ended in 1865.

Antiwar spirit was strongest in the Midwest, especially in Indiana and Illinois, where secret groups formed. The largest group was known as the Knights of the Golden Circle. The Knights, and groups like them, had secret handshakes and passwords. They met in the dark of the night. The members of these groups were known as Copperheads, after one of the four poisonous snakes living in North America. Some Copperheads and Confederate agents made plans for ending the war so that the South would win.

During the first half of 1864, when the war was going badly for the North, the Copperhead movement grew to its greatest strength. Then the Union army won some important victories. After Lincoln was reelected in November, the antiwar movement died out.

Both the Union and the Confederate governments tried to control people who were against the war. They were afraid that antiwar groups would convince men to stop fighting.

In the North, people against the war urged men to refuse to go into the army. They urged soldiers to desert. In September 1862, Lincoln issued a proclamation that took away freedom of speech and freedom from arrest without a quick trial. "All persons discouraging volunteer enlistment, resisting militia drafts, or guilty of any disloyal practice" could be arrested. Several hundred people who spoke against the draft or against the war were jailed. They included five

In both the North and the South, people who spoke against the war could be arrested and jailed. Above is an illustration of a prison in New York where antiwar prisoners were held.

New Yorkers gather at a newspaper office, opposite, to read the latest headlines about the war.

newspaper editors who published antiwar articles, three judges, and some minor political leaders.

The Confederate government required civilians and soldiers on leave to carry passports anywhere near a battlefield or army camp. A person caught without a passport could be thrown into jail. Many people bought or made fake passports. President Davis, like Lincoln in the North, allowed people who spoke against the war to be arrested and jailed without a trial. Secret groups of antiwar and pro-Union Southerners formed in parts of the Confederacy. They had such names as the Peace Society, the Heroes of America, and the Peace and Constitution Society.

News from the Front

The people back home wanted to know what was happening on Civil War battlefields. Civilians waited anxiously for soldiers' letters. They waited at the newspaper offices for the latest newspaper to go on sale. They looked forward to articles about how the war was going and to drawings of battles. But they especially wanted to see the lists of casualties printed in the local papers. If they didn't see the name of their loved one on the list, they knew he was safe until the next battle.

PICTURES OF THE CIVIL WAR

Photographers visited army camps and took pictures of Civil War soldiers, which the soldiers then sent home to their families. Camera equipment was bulky and heavy. A person being photographed had to stay still for about thirty seconds, or the photograph would be blurred.

Mathew Brady and his assistants were among the first photographers to travel with the Union armies. War photographers traveled with a camera, a large, heavy box on legs, and a darkroom—a tent on a wagon—where they developed the photographs. They could not take pictures of the battles, because cameras of the time were too slow to capture action on film. Photographers sometimes got shot at because they couldn't move their equipment out of the way fast enough. Mathew Brady later said, "No one will ever know what I went through to secure [get] those negatives." He and his assistants took more than 3,500 pictures during the Civil War. Their photographs of dead soldiers after the battles shocked the people back home.

Artists also traveled with the armies to draw pictures of battles and soldiers. Alfred Waud and Winslow Homer became famous for the pictures they drew for newspapers such as *Harper's Weekly* and *Frank Leslie's Illustrated Newspaper*. Newspapers could not yet reprint photographs.

Photographer Mathew Brady's wagon darkroom and his assistants, in the field with the Union army near Petersburg, Virginia, 1864

Newspapers in the North and South reported in detail on what the armies were doing. Generals on both sides complained that the newspapers gave away useful information to the enemy about how many soldiers were marching and where they were going. But most newspaper editors felt it was their duty to report everything they found out. One Southern editor even printed war news that he got from Northern papers.

Newspapers in both the North and South printed articles that argued against the war, criticized their governments, and gave away important information about their armies' actions. The Union government forced dozens of Union newspapers to close down. In 1863 Southern newspapers formed a group that successfully bargained with the Confederate government to let them keep some freedom of the press. Not all newspapers criticized the war. Most newspapers tried to urge people to be patriotic and support the war. The papers also continued with the job of entertaining people. They printed poems, jokes, and funny stories to help distract people from worries about the war.

Southern newspapers suffered from paper shortages. Before the war, they had gotten their paper from the North. Southern paper mills were too few to supply paper for all the newspapers. Ink was also hard to get in the South. One paper used shoe polish as a substitute. Because of shortages, about one-half of all the newspapers in the South went out of business during the war.

Passing the Time

In spite of the war, people tried to enjoy life. Richer people kept up the social life they had before the war. The daughter of a plantation

President Lincoln, left, *reads with his nine-year-old son, Thomas "Tad" Lincoln, in 1864. Lincoln's twelve-year-old son Willie died in the White House in 1862.*

owner in Virginia wrote in September 1861, "We have a delightful day for our trip, called in Salem and spent an hour with Addie who begged me to stay all day with her. We reached Ivy Hill at four, where we met with Cousin Emma and made two new [friends]. . . . Two gentlemen came in this evening . . . Kate gave me her soldier brother, [I] liked him very much but not enough to win him and claim him for my better half."

Rich Northern people also enjoyed the good

The Union's first lady, Mary Todd Lincoln, above, *received criticism from some Northerners for wearing beautiful and expensive clothing during the war. She was a Southerner who had four brothers fighting for the South.*

life. In New York, the wife of a judge wrote, "went . . . to the different artists' studios. . . . We saw fine sketches of Indians from Lake Superior, many pleasing scenes from New England life, some fine old cabinets. . . . Last evening we went to Judge Bell's; the day before to a musical matinee at Mrs. James Brooks'; Tuesday to a grand entertainment at Mr. Francis Cutting's. . . . "

In the larger towns and cities of the North and South, going to plays was a popular activity. Some of the plays were serious, often tragedies by William Shakespeare. But the war itself was so serious that most people wanted to see something happier. Theaters most often presented comedies and musicals. Because there were few men at home in the South, women dressed like men to play many of the male parts.

Getting together to play music and to sing songs was a favorite part of everyday life all over Civil War America. People bought sheet music so they could play and sing songs at home. The sheet music for the most popular songs, such as "When This Cruel War Is Over," sold thousands of copies.

In the South, poor people had little time for play and fun. Still, entertainers—jugglers, tumblers, dancers, and musicians—continued to travel from town to town. Minstrel shows are groups of usually white comics made up to look black, who sing, dance, and joke. Some had black performers. The shows continued to travel through the South and attract large crowds. Towns and villages also arranged special events to support the soldiers. These events included popular entertainment. Country dwellers eagerly traveled into town to attend these events.

An example of sheet music sold during the Civil War

57

Southern farm folk shared work at corn-shucking or quilting and spinning bees. In the summer, religious camp meetings gave farm folk a chance to socialize with people from other places. Whenever Confederate soldiers came home, they visited their neighbors, friends, and sweethearts. Southern society did not think that young ladies should travel without a man as an escort, or protector. Because most young Southern men were in the army, younger teenaged boys had to escort young ladies. A teenaged boy wrote to a soldier, "I went to [a meeting]...and coming home I had to keep company with about a dozen girls.... Come home and help me out for I tell you that I have my hands full."

In the Southern countryside, people continued to fish and hunt for food as well as for pleasure. Games such as chess and checkers were also popular. A shortage of playing cards meant card games became less frequent. Sometimes blockade-runners delivered playing cards to Southern ports. In June 1864, a South Carolina newspaper reported the arrival of sets of playing cards. The cards showed Confederate generals and politicians instead of kings and queens.

In rural Northern places, country fairs had always been popular. Northern folk tried to continue the fairs during the war. Crawford County, Ohio, made a big effort in 1861 to have a normal fair. A local newspaper urged, "Every one can do something to make our Fair more attractive." But some people thought it was wrong to have a fair when a war was going on. So, few people exhibited their farm animals, fruits, and vegetables. No farm machinery or flower arrangements were shown. Other fair organizers made changes. The state fair in

Union infantrymen pose for a photograph in their camp. Life in camp could be lonely, especially for the men who had families at home.

Illinois, for example, offered prizes for the best gun exhibits and the best collections of war trophies, in addition to the regular exhibits of farm products.

Farming communities in the North continued the tradition of the Saturday night dance. All that was needed was a room, either a meeting hall or a barn, and a fiddle player. A midwesterner remembered, "It was a joy to watch him [the fiddle player] start the set . . . he took his seat in a big chair. . . . One mighty stomp of his boot . . . a slicing sweep of his bow across the taut strings, and a command of 'Honors tew your partners'. . . and the dance began."

Northerners celebrated the Fourth of July with great enthusiasm during the war. Every town and village had speeches, parades, and picnics. But holidays such as Christmas were often very sad for families in the North and South. Many families had recently learned of the death of a loved one. Many other families were too poor to celebrate very much.

Still, families made the best of a difficult time. On December 26, 1862, a North Carolina woman wrote to her soldier husband, "Our children had no Christmas tree . . . but they hung up their stockings and were much pleased with their [gifts]—cake, sugar, candy (home-made), an apple apiece, nuts, etc. The fire crackers from dear papa pleased them better than anything else." A young woman on a still-wealthy Virginia plantation wrote in her diary on Christmas Day 1862, "Christmas, but not as of old. The merry holidays that once were have given place to sad and gloomy pleasures." Her words might have been written by any American, Northerner or Southerner.

Patriotic Words and Music

During the Civil War, composers, authors, and

poets all made the Civil War their subject. People composed patriotic songs, songs about battles, love songs, and songs about soldiers wishing to come home. Poets and writers created poems about the battles and books and stories about the war.

After visiting a Union army camp in 1861, Julia Ward Howe wrote the "Battle Hymn of the Republic." The song begins with an image of Union soldiers fighting on God's side to free the slaves.

Mine eyes have seen the glory of the coming of the Lord:
He is trampling out the vintage where the grapes of wrath are stored,
He hath loosed the fateful lightning of his terrible swift sword:
His truth is marching on.

Walt Whitman was already a famous poet when the war began. He visited wounded Union soldiers in the hospital. He wrote several books of poems about his wartime hospital experiences and about the Civil War. One of Whitman's poems, about a family receiving news of their soldier son's death, begins:

Come up from the fields father, here's a letter from our Pete,
And come to the front door mother, here's a letter from thy dear son. . . .

Louisa May Alcott became famous for her book *Little Women*, which she wrote after the Civil War. During the war, she had worked as a nurse and caught typhoid at the hospital. She never fully recovered and was too weak to go back to work. She wrote to try to

Walt Whitman began visiting hospitalized wounded soldiers in 1862 after his brother was wounded at the Battle of Fredericksburg that same year. He bought small presents for both Union and Confederate patients.

support herself and her family while her father went to war. *Little Women* is the story of a Northern mother and her daughters and how they lived while their father was away serving as an army chaplain.

The poet Sidney Lanier of Georgia said that the Civil War was good for Southern literature because it gave people something important to write about. Also, the blockade cut off supplies of new books from the North and Europe. So Southerners wrote and published much more than they had before the war. They saw it as their duty to encourage their readers to believe in the righteousness of the Southern cause. Authors such as William Gilmore Simms of South Carolina and Augusta Jane Evans of Alabama became famous in the South. Simms's most famous book was his biography of the great Confederate general Stonewall Jackson. Evans wrote a novel about the war, which she dedicated to "the Brave Soldiers of the Southern Army."

The most famous Southern patriotic song was "Dixie." (Dixie had become the nickname for the South.) An Ohioan, Dan Emmet, wrote "Dixie" just before the war. He used the song in his

Louisa May Alcott

traveling minstrel show. During the war, both sides played and sang the song. President Lincoln particularly enjoyed it. "Dixie" speaks of the Southerners' love of their land:

I wish I was in Dixie,
Hooray! Hooray!
In Dixie Land, I'll take my stand,
To live and die in Dixie.

Spirituals expressed the suffering of slaves and their longing for freedom. Some began as chants called from one slave to another as they worked in the fields. Such songs had been passed on from one slave to another for many years. The coming of the Civil War led to the creation of new spirituals. Several slaves were thrown into jail for singing a song with the words "we'll fight for liberty."

The most popular song in both the North and the South was "When This Cruel War Is Over." Singers changed one word, singing "in your suit of blue" or "in your suit of grey," depending which side they were on. One million copies of the sheet music were sold. Another popular song for both sides, "Tenting on the Old Campground," described a camp after a battle:

We've been fighting today on the old
* campground*
Many are lying near;
Some are dead and some are dying,
Many are in tears.

The song's chorus spoke about how hard the war was for everyone:

Many are the hearts that are weary tonight,
Wishing for the war to cease.

A scene of homecoming, opposite. A soldier wrote, "As I look back I am bewildered when I think of the hundreds of miles I have tramped, the thousands of dead and wounded that I have seen, and the many strange sights that I have witnessed. I can truly thank God for his . . . care over me."

Soldiers and civilians, Union and Confederate, all grew weary of the war. A Union soldier, who could have been speaking for all soldiers, wrote to his wife, "What a good sound there is to the word home . . . I think that we shall all know how to value it if we ever get there."

Vicksburg: Life in a City under Siege

In May 1863, General Grant's Union army surrounded Vicksburg, Mississippi. They used big guns called siege guns to bombard the city. For the people living in this Southern town, normal life stopped. There were no open stores, hotels, or places to eat. No longer could people do normal things to relax. Children could not play outside. Adults could not walk in the street.

Shells fired from the Union guns fell everywhere in the city. When the bombardment began, people hid in their basements. Mrs. William Lord, her five children, and the family's slaves were in their basement one night. The exploding shells shook the ground. The slaves began moaning and praying. Four-year-old Lida began to cry. Her mother tried to comfort her. She said, "Don't cry, my darling, God will protect us." "But mamma," sobbed Lida, "I's so 'fraid God's killed too!"

Many people dug caves for shelter. They lived in the caves week after week. They were lucky if they got a chance to take a bath once every two weeks. People built small stoves at the fronts of the caves. When the shelling stopped, they used these stoves to cook. Then, when the shelling began again, everyone went back inside the cave. Sometimes twenty-four hours went by before people in the caves had a chance to cook.

The Confederate soldiers defending the city got the best food because they needed energy to fight. Yet even the soldiers were starving. Each soldier got a small wheat, pea, or rice biscuit, bread, and a square-inch piece of meat each day. The civilians got even less.

Everyone, rich and poor, black and white, child and adult, struggled to survive. The price for a barrel of flour rose to 1,000 Confederate dollars. As the days passed, the price no longer mattered because there was no flour to buy. People went to the edge of the Mississippi River and cut thorny blackberry canes. They boiled the canes to make them soft and then ate them. They made a soup out of wild parsley, onion grass, and water. People ate rats. The army killed its mules for food and gave civilians the meat. But it tasted so bad that many people could not eat it.

At one cave, a woman named Mary Loughborough and her young daughter were hungry, sick, and tired. A Confederate soldier brought the girl a gift, a tame bird, to play with. The sick girl played with it a while and then became tired again. The family's cook, a female slave, said, "Miss Mary, she's hungry; let me make her some soup from the bird." Mary Loughborough wrote in her diary, "The next time [the cook] appeared, it was with a cup of soup, and a little plate, on which lay the white meat of the poor little bird."

Vicksburg finally surrendered on July 4, 1863. The siege had lasted for six weeks. Maggie Lord's husband "came into the cave, pale as death and with such a look of agony on his face, as I would wish never to see again, [he] said 'Maggie take the children home directly, the town is surrendered. . . .' I was speechless with grief, no one spoke, even the poor children were silent. . . . As I started up the hill with the children, the tears began to flow and all the weary way home, I wept. . . . At last we reached the house. . . . The dressing room was in ruins, the end where the fireplace had been was blown entirely out. The nursery [had a deep hole] in the middle of the floor, every room in the house injured. . . . You can imagine our feelings when the U.S. Army entered, their banners flying and their hateful tunes sounding in our ears."

The bombardment wrecked many houses but killed only about twelve civilians. Many more were so weak from hunger that they died later from disease. The people of Vicksburg did not forget their suffering during the Siege of Vicksburg. For the next eighty-two years, the city of Vicksburg refused to celebrate the Fourth of July.

Union soldiers lived in a complex system of underground burrows during the Siege of Vicksburg.

Time Line

February 4–9, 1861: Southern states that have seceded (withdrawn) from the United States of America adopt a new constitution, elect Jefferson Davis president, and form the Confederate States of America.

April 12, 1861: The Civil War begins as Confederate forces open fire on Fort Sumter in Charleston Harbor, South Carolina. People on both sides believe that the war will end quickly and gloriously. These hopes are soon dashed as news of the first battles of 1861 reaches the home front.

April 19, 1861: President Lincoln announces a naval blockade of Southern ports. By 1864 the Union blockade stops one ship in three from entering Southern ports. A hardship on Southerners, the blockade forces the South to increase its own manufacturing capacity.

April 16, 1862: The Confederate Congress passes a draft law, which is the first such law in American history. Many Southerners object to the law, which allows wealthy men to avoid being drafted into army service.

September 22, 1862: President Lincoln issues the Emancipation Proclamation to free the slaves in the rebel states. It will take effect on January 1, 1863. Lincoln is called the "Great Emancipator," but the proclamation will have little effect on the lives of Southern slaves until after the war.

March 3, 1863: U.S. Congress passes the Enrollment Act (draft law). Much like the Confederate draft law, the Enrollment Act allows men to pay their way out of service in the army. Because of this, many Northern citizens strongly oppose it.

April 2, 1863: Richmond Bread Riot. About one thousand hungry people in Richmond, Virginia—angry about high food prices—break into shops and steal food. President Davis, accompanied by armed troops, orders the rioters off.

May 22–July 4, 1863: The Siege of Vicksburg. Capturing this city allows the North to control the Mississippi River and the territory on the western side of the river. The Mississippi is a major trade route, and Southern families on the home front suffer from shortages of food and supplies.

July 13–16, 1863: New York City Draft Riots. A mob of white people, angry about the draft, attack black people and wreck buildings. Union soldiers finally break up the riot.

November 8, 1864: Lincoln is reelected president of the United States, dashing Southern hopes for a negotiated end to the Civil War.

November 15–December 10, 1864: Sherman's March to the Sea. Union troops commanded by General William T. Sherman march from Atlanta to Savannah, Georgia, destroying food and property in an effort to break the spirit of Southerners.

April 9–June 2, 1865: The Civil War comes to an end as the Confederate armies throughout the South surrender. By the time the war is over, 260,000 Confederate soldiers and 360,000 Union soldiers have died. The war has also left in ruins farms and cities wherever fighting occurred.

Notes

For quoted material in text:

p. 15, George Winston Smith and Charles Judah, *Life in the North During the Civil War: A Source History* (Albuquerque: University of New Mexico Press, 1966), 204.

p. 16, Charles F. Larimer, ed., *Love and Valor: Intimate Civil War Letters Between Captain Jacob and Emeline Ritner* (Western Springs, IL: Sigourney Press, 2000), 164.

p. 16, Smith and Judah, *Life in the North During the Civil War*, 167.

p. 17, Nina Silber and Mary Beth Sievens, eds., *Yankee Correspondence: Civil War Letters between New England Soldiers and the Home Front* (Charlottesville: University Press of Virginia, 1996), 135.

p. 17, Timothy Levi Biel, *Life in the North During the Civil War* (San Diego: Lucent Books, 1997), 51.

p. 17, Silber and Sievens, eds., *Yankee Correspondence*, 146–147.

p. 17, James Marten, *The Children's Civil War* (Chapel Hill: University of North Carolina Press, 1998), 174.

p. 17, Norman Bolotin and Angela Herb, *For Home and Country: A Civil War Scrapbook* (New York: Dutton, 1995), 38.

p. 26, John Gallatin Paxton, ed., *The Civil War Letters of General Frank "Bull" Paxton, CSA, a Lieutenant of Lee and Jackson* (Hillsboro, TX: Hill Jr. College Press, 1978), 73.

pp. 26–27, Adeline Hodges, interviewed, in *The American Slave: A Composite Autobiography*, ed. George P. Rawick, vol. 6, *Alabama and Indiana Narratives* (Westport, CT: Greenwood Publishing Co., 1972), 181.

p. 31, James M. McPherson, *Battle Cry of Freedom: The Civil War Era* (New York: Oxford University Press, 1988), 441.

p. 31, Bolotin and Herb, *For Home and Country* (New York: Dutton, 1995), 33.

p. 31, Bell Irvin Wiley, *Embattled Confederates* (New York: Bonanza Books, 1964), 115.

p. 31, Emmy E. Werner, *Reluctant Witnesses: Children's Voices from the Civil War* (Boulder, CO: Westview Press, 1998), 110.

p. 33, Marten, *The Children's Civil War*, 101.

p. 34, Werner, *Reluctant Witnesses*, 107.

p. 34, Delia Garlic, interviewed, in *The American Slave: A Composite Autobiography*, ed. George P. Rawick, vol. 6, *Alabama and Indiana Narratives* (Westport, CT: Greenwood Publishing Co., 1972), 131.

pp. 34–35, Walter Calloway, interviewed, in *The American Slave: A Composite Autobiography*, George P. Rawick, vol. 6, *Alabama and Indiana Narratives* (Westport, CT: Greenwood Publishing Co., 1972), 53.

p. 35, Hannah Jones, interviewed, in *The American Slave: A Composite Autobiography*, ed. George P. Rawick, vol. 6, *Alabama and Indiana Narratives* (Westport, CT: Greenwood Publishing Co., 1972), 239–240.

p. 35, Wiley, *Embattled Confederates*, 236.

p. 35, Silber and Sievens, eds., *Yankee Correspondence*, 108.

p. 36, Walter Sullivan, ed., *The War the Women Lived: Female Voices from the Confederate South* (Nashville: J. S. Sanders & Co., 1995), 153.

p. 38, J. J. Kellogg, *The Vicksburg Campaign and Reminiscences* (Washington, IA: Evening Journal, 1913), 50–51.

p. 38, John C. Pemberton, *Pemberton: Defender of Vicksburg* (Chapel Hill: University of North Carolina Press, 1942), 24.

p. 39, Dale E. Floyd, ed., *"Dear Friends at Home . . . ": The Letters and Diary of Thomas James Owen, Fiftieth New York Volunteer Engineer Regiment, During the Civil War* (Washington, D.C.: Government Printing Office, 1985), 80.

p. 43, Bell Irvin Wiley, *The Life of Johnny Reb: The Common Soldier of the Confederacy* (Baton Rouge: Louisiana State University Press, 1986), 263.

pp. 44–45, Silber and Sievens, eds., *Yankee Correspondence*, 60.

p. 45, Larimer, ed., *Love and Valor*, 87.

p. 45, McPherson, *Battle Cry of Freedom*, 493.

p. 45, Bruce Catton, *The American Heritage New History of the Civil War* (New York: Viking, 1996), 135.

p. 46, Silber and Sievens, eds., *Yankee Correspondence*, 86.

p. 48, Steven A. Channing, *Confederate Ordeal: The Southern Home Front* (Alexandria, VA: Time-Life Books, 1984), 77.

p. 51, Maria Lydig Daly, *Diary of a Union Lady, 1861-1865*, ed. Harold Earl Hammond (Lincoln: University of Nebraska Press, 2000), 246.

p. 52, McPherson, *Battle Cry of Freedom*, 493.

p. 56, Nancy Chappelear Baird, ed., *Journals of Amanda Virginia Edmonds, Lass of the Mosby Confederacy, 1859–1867* (Stephens City, VA: Commercial Press, 1984), 58.

p. 57, Daly, *Diary of a Union Lady*, ed. Hammond, 217–218.

p. 58, Wiley, *Embattled Confederates*, 173.

p. 58, Smith and Judah, *Life in the North During the Civil War*, 263.

p. 59, Biel, *Life in the North During the Civil War*, 70.

p. 59, Wiley, *Embattled Confederates*, 126.

p. 59, Baird, ed., *Journals of Amanda Virginia Edmonds*, 129.

p. 60, Julia Ward Howe, "Battle Hymn of the Republic," in *The Photographic History of the Civil War*, Francis Trevelyan Miller, vol. 9, *Poetry and Eloquence from the Blue and the Gray* (New York: Thomas Yoseloff, 1957), 156.

p. 60, Walt Whitman, "Come Up From the Fields Father," in *Annals of America*, vol. 9 (Chicago: Encyclopaedia Britannica, Inc., 1976), 559.

p. 61, Channing, *Confederate Ordeal*, 46.

p. 62, Dan Emmet, "Dixie," in *The Photographic History of the Civil War*, Francis Trevelyan Miller, vol. 9, *Poetry and Eloquence from the Blue and the Gray* (New York: Thomas Yoseloff, 1957), 164.

p. 62, "We'll Soon Be Free," in *The Photographic History of the Civil War*, Francis Trevelyan Miller, vol. 9, *Poetry and Eloquence from the Blue and the Gray* (New York: Thomas Yoseloff, 1957), 352.

p. 62, Charles Carroll Sawyer, "When This Cruel War Is Over," in *The Photographic History of the Civil War*, Francis Trevelyan Miller, vol. 9, *Poetry and Eloquence from the Blue and the Gray* (New York: Thomas Yoseloff, 1957), 351.

p. 62, Walter Kittredge, "Tenting on the Old Campground," in *The Photographic History of the Civil War*, Francis Trevelyan Miller, vol. 9, *Poetry and Eloquence from the Blue and the Gray* (New York: Thomas Yoseloff, 1957), 348.

p. 63, Silber and Sievens, eds., *Yankee Correspondence*, 157.

For material quoted in sidebars:

p. 21, Callie Williams, interviewed, in *The American Slave: A Composite Autobiography*, ed. George P. Rawick, vol. 6, *Alabama and Indiana Narratives* (Westport, CT: Greenwood Publishing Co., 1972), 427.

p. 24, Wiley, *Embattled Confederates*, 78.

p. 33, Wayne D. Rasmussen, ed., *Agriculture in the United States: A Documentary History*, vol. 1 (New York: Random House, 1975), 677.

p. 54, Roy Meredith, *Mr. Lincoln's Camera Man* (New York: Charles Scribner's Sons, 1946), vii.

p. 64, Werner, *Reluctant Witnesses*, 81.

p. 64, Mary Loughborough, *My Cave Life in Vicksburg* (Little Rock, AR: Kellogg Printing Company, 1882), 137.

p. 65, Werner, *Reluctant Witnesses*, 90.

For material quoted in captions:

p. 32, Marten, *The Children's Civil War*, 145.

p. 34, Ibid., 114.

p. 35, Mary Ella Grandberry, interviewed, in *The American Slave: A Composite Autobiography*, ed. George P. Rawick, vol. 6, *Alabama and Indiana Narratives* (Westport, CT: Greenwood Publishing Co., 1972), 163.

p. 40, Bolotin and Herb, *For Home and Country*, 55.

p. 50, Francis A. Lord, *They Fought for the Union*, (New York: Bonanza Books, 1960), 5.

p. 62, Robert Hunt Rhodes, ed., *All for the Union: The Civil War Diary and Letters of Elisha Hunt Rhodes* (New York: Orion Books, 1991), 93.

Selected Bibliography

Biel, Timothy Levi. *Life in the North During the Civil War*. San Diego: Lucent Books, 1997.

Channing, Steven A. *Confederate Ordeal: The Southern Home Front*. Alexandria, VA: Time-Life Books, 1984.

Daly, Maria Lydig. *Diary of a Union Lady, 1861-1865*. Lincoln: University of Nebraska Press, 2000.

Larimer, Charles F., ed. *Love and Valor: Intimate Civil War Letters Between Captain Jacob and Emeline Ritner*. Western Springs, IL: Sigourney Press, 2000.

Marten, James. *The Children's Civil War*. Chapel Hill: University of North Carolina Press, 1998.

McPherson, James M. *Battle Cry of Freedom: The Civil War Era.* New York: Oxford University Press, 1988.

Silber, Nina, and Mary Beth Sievens, eds. *Yankee Correspondence: Civil War Letters between New England Soldiers and the Home Front*. Charlottesville: University Press of Virginia, 1996.

Smith, Carter, ed. *Behind the Lines: A Sourcebook on the Civil War*. Brookfield, CT: Millbrook Press, 1993.

Smith, George Winston, and Charles Judah. *Life in the North During the Civil War: A Source History*. Albuquerque: University of New Mexico Press, 1966.

Sullivan, Walter, ed. *The War the Women Lived: Female Voices from the Confederate South*. Nashville: J. S. Sanders & Co., 1995.

Werner, Emmy E. *Reluctant Witnesses: Children's Voices from the Civil War*. Boulder, CO: Westview Press, 1998.

For More Information

Books

Beller, Susan Provost. *Confederate Ladies of Richmond*. Brookfield, CT: Twenty-First Century Books, 1999.

Burchard, Peter. *Lincoln and Slavery*. New York: Atheneum, 1999.

Clinton, Catherine. *Scholastic Encyclopedia of the Civil War*. New York: Scholastic, Inc., 1999.

Damon, Duane. *When This Cruel War Is Over: The Civil War Home Front*. Minneapolis: Lerner Publications, 1996.

Day, Nancy. *Your Travel Guide to Civil War America*. Minneapolis: Runestone Press, 2001.

Greene, Meg. *Slave Young, Slave Long: The American Slave Experience*. Minneapolis: Lerner Publications, 1999.

Ransom, Candace F. *Children of the Civil War*. Minneapolis: Carolrhoda Books, 1998.

Stanchak, John. *Civil War*. New York: Dorling Kindersley, 2000.

Whitelaw, Nancy. *Clara Barton: Civil War Nurse*. Springfield, NJ: Enslow Publishers, 1997.

Videos

The Civil War. Walpole, NH: Florentine Films, 1990. Videocassette series. This PBS series by Ken Burns and narrated by David McCullough includes personal accounts and archival photos, as well as commentary by many writers on the period.

The Gettysburg Civilians. New York: A & E Networks, 1993. Includes diaries, photos, and reenactments of battles from the civilian's point of view.

Web Sites

<http://www.ajkids.com>
  Users can ask questions about U.S. history in plain language and get connected to several different sites with answers.

<http://valley.vcdh.virginia.edu>
  "The Valley of the Shadow: Two Communities in the American Civil War"; letters, diaries, and newspaper articles about life in a Pennsylvania community and a Virginia community

<http://digital.nypl.org/schomburg/images_aa19/>
  Images of African Americans from the nineteenth century; magazine illustrations of black Americans, including Civil War troops

<http://www.cwc.lsu.edu/BeyondFaceValue>
  Pictures of slaves at work, which were once used on Confederate money

Places to Visit

Carter's Grove, Williamsburg, Virginia: the mansion and slave quarters of a plantation that once covered three hundred thousand acres and had one thousand slaves

Museum of the Confederacy, Richmond, Virginia: paintings, clothing and uniforms, weapons, battle flags. The White House of the Confederacy is next door.

Jennie Wade House and Schriver House, both in Gettysburg, Pennsylvania: homes of local civilians during the Battle of Gettysburg

Index

About the Authors

James R. Arnold was born in Illinois, and his family moved to Switzerland when he was a teenager. His fascination with the history of war was born on the battlefields of Europe. He returned to the United States for his college education. For the past twenty-five years, he and his wife, Roberta Wiener, have lived and farmed in the Shenandoah Valley of Virginia and toured all the Civil War battlefields.

Mr. Arnold's great-great-grandfather was shot and killed in Fairfax, Virginia, because he voted against secession. Another ancestor served in an Ohio regiment during the Civil War. Mr. Arnold has written more than twenty books about American and European wars, and he has contributed to many others.

Roberta Wiener grew up in Pennsylvania and completed her education in Washington, D.C. After many years of touring battlefields and researching books with her husband, James R. Arnold, she has said, "The more I learn about war, the more fascinating it becomes." Ms. Wiener has coauthored nine books with Mr. Arnold and edited numerous educational books, including a children's encyclopedia. She has also worked as an archivist for the U.S. Army.

><del>++</del>+<del>+</del>O<del>+</del><del>+</del>+<del>+</del>+<del>+</del>+<

Picture Acknowledgments